THE HUMAN PATH ACROSS THE CONTINENTS

PATHWAYS THROUGH NORTH AMERICA

Cynthia O'Brien

CRABTREE
PUBLISHING COMPANY
WWW.CRABTREEBOOKS.COM

CRABTREE
PUBLISHING COMPANY
WWW.CRABTREEBOOKS.COM

Author: Cynthia O'Brien

Editorial director: Kathy Middleton

Editors: Rachel Cooke, Janine Deschenes

Design: Jeni Child

Photo research:
FFP Consulting; Tammy McGarr

Proofreader: Melissa Boyce

Prepress and production coordinator: Tammy McGarr

Print coordinator: Katherine Berti

Produced for Crabtree Publishing Company by
FFP Consulting Limited

Images:
t=Top, b=Bottom, tl=Top Left, tr=Top Right, bl=Bottom Left, br=Bottom Right, c=Center, lc=Left Center, rc=Right Center

Alamy
  Jerry Kobalenko: p. 11t; Archie Fusilero: p. 13b; FEMA: p. 15t;
  Nick Suydam: p. 20b; World Pictures: p. 26b; Keith Dannemiller: p. 27b
Shutterstock
  Josef Hanus: p. 6b; SeaRick1: p. 7l; mikecphoto: p. 12b; LesPalenik: p. 13t;
  Jon Nicholls Photography: p. 17tr; Darryl Brooks: p. 18–19b;
  Ancha Chiangmai: p. 19t; Eric Valenne geostory: p. 19lc;
  Julien Hautcoeur: p. 22b; Malachi Jacobs: p. 23t; trekandshoot: p. 25t;
  Walter Cicchetti: p. 25lc; ChameleonsEye: p. 27 tr; Lissandra Melo: p. 31
AMTRAK: p. 21b
Cirium/Delta: p. 18t
Matt Donnelly: California Zephyr: cover
Toronto Transit Commission: p. 12t
Wikimedia: p. 5br

All other images from Shutterstock

Maps: Jeni Child

Library and Archives Canada Cataloguing in Publication

Title: Pathways through North America / Cynthia O'Brien.
Names: O'Brien, Cynthia (Cynthia J.), author.
Description: Series statement: The human path across the continents |
  Includes index.
Identifiers: Canadiana (print) 20190112107 | Canadiana (ebook) 20190112115
  ISBN 9780778766421 (hardcover)
  ISBN 9780778766490 (softcover)
  ISBN 9781427124012 (HTML)
Subjects: LCSH: Human ecology—North America—Juvenile literature. |
  LCSH: North America—Juvenile literature.
Classification: LCC GF501 .O27 2019 | DDC j304.2097—dc23

Library of Congress Cataloging-in-Publication Data

Names: O'Brien, Cynthia (Cynthia J.), author.
Title: Pathways through North America / Cynthia O'Brien.
Description: New York : Crabtree Publishing Company, [2020] |
  Series: The human path across the continents | Includes index.
Identifiers: LCCN 2019023328 (print) | LCCN 2019023329 (ebook) |
  ISBN 9780778766421 (hardcover) |
  ISBN 9780778766490 (paperback) |
  ISBN 9781427124012 (ebook)
Subjects: LCSH: Human ecology--North America--Juvenile literature. |
  Nature--Effect of human beings on--North America--Juvenile literature. |
  Physical geography--North America--Juvenile literature. |
  North America--Environmental conditions--Juvenile literature.
Classification: LCC GF501 .O37 2020 (print) | LCC GF501 (ebook) |
  DDC 304.2097--dc23
LC record available at https://lccn.loc.gov/2019023328
LC ebook record available at https://lccn.loc.gov/2019023329

Crabtree Publishing Company
www.crabtreebooks.com   1-800-387-7650

Printed in the U.S.A./082019/CG20190712

Published in Canada
Crabtree Publishing
616 Welland Ave.
St. Catharines, Ontario
L2M 5V6

Published in the United States
Crabtree Publishing
PMB 59051
350 Fifth Avenue, 59th Floor
New York, New York 10118

Published in the United Kingdom
Crabtree Publishing
Maritime House
Basin Road North, Hove
BN41 1WR

Published in Australia
Crabtree Publishing
Unit 3–5 Currumbin Court
Capalaba
QLD 4157

CONTENTS

NORTH AMERICA

The Human Path Across
NORTH AMERICA

GREENLAND

ALASKA

CANADA

UNITED STATES
OF AMERICA

Taos Pueblo

Austin

ATLANTIC OCEAN

MEXICO

CARIBBEAN ISLANDS

BELIZE — HONDURAS

— NICARAGUA

GUATEMALA

EL SALVADOR

PACIFIC OCEAN

COSTA RICA

PANAMA

The continent of North America stretches from Greenland's icy arctic to the tropical rain forests in Panama. It includes hot deserts and towering mountains. The journeys in this book include a cross-country road trip, a flight across the United States, and a trek across Navajo tribal lands. These and other paths across North America help show how humans affect, and are affected by, the environments in which they live.

▶ **TAOS PUEBLO,** New Mexico, is one of the oldest settlements in North America that is still lived in today. The Taos Pueblo people have made it their home for more than 1,000 years. **Indigenous** peoples began arriving in North America at least 15,000 years ago. Some may have traveled over a land bridge that formed between Asia and North America near the end of the last **Ice Age.** Others may have traveled by boat to the Pacific or Atlantic coasts. People used river systems and found land routes to travel, hunt, and trade with one another. Later, when European **settlers** reached North America, their way of life changed.

AUSTIN, TEXAS first grew up in the 1800s on the Colorado River, which gave it a water source and transportation links. Today, Austin is one of the fastest-growing cities in North America. People are attracted by its strong **economy**. The founding of towns and cities such as Austin was part of the European settlement of North America that began in the 1600s. Moving west, these settlers claimed land for farming across the continent. This forced many Indigenous peoples onto **reservations** and **reserves**.

The city of Austin, Texas

IN 1869, WORKERS CELEBRATED when the railway from the East to the West Coast of the United States was completed. In 1885, workers finished the railway that connected eastern Canada to the West. Transportation links like these helped North America's towns and cities grow, especially on the East and West Coasts. For the first time, people and goods could be transported quickly across the continent. Airports and highways created more ways to travel. Though these transportation routes helped populate much of North America, few people today live in the continent's extreme **climates** and landscapes.

Taos Pueblo, New Mexico

The East-West railway opens, 1869

Ferry From SEATTLE

A sea journey along the northwestern coast of North America travels more than 850 miles (1,368 km), past islands and mountains. Major coastal cities include Seattle in the United States and Vancouver in Canada, but the coast also has many smaller settlements. Some of these places are more easily accessed by sea than by road, so ferry travel is important in this region.

Ferry leaving Vancouver

↓ VANCOUVER IS A PORT CITY because of its location on the Pacific coast. Goods from here are **imported** and **exported**, especially to Asia and the United States. Ferries and cruise ships also leave from here.

Like many settlements along this coast, Vancouver grew up when early settlers arrived from Europe and Russia. They were drawn by the land and its rich **natural resources**. Coastal cities grew around the fishing, shipping, mining, and lumber **industries** that are still important today.

BRITISH COLUMBIA

ALASKA

Vancouver

Sidney
Victoria

Anacortes

Port Angeles

Seattle

WASHINGTON

—— Ferry crossings

CANADA

Haida Gwaii

VANCOUVER

SEATTLE

UNITED STATES

HAIDA TOTEM CARVINGS are famous. Some can be seen in Stanley Park, Vancouver. You can travel from there by ferry to the islands of Haida Gwaii where they came from. These islands are off the coast of British Columbia, Canada. They are the traditional homelands of the Haida people, who came to the region long before European settlers, living off the plentiful food of the ocean and rivers. Unlike many **First Nations**, the Haida people did not sign a **treaty** and did not move from their lands. Today, the Haida govern themselves and make their living through tourism, fishing, and lumber. All along this coast, people now work to protect the wildlife from the impact of growing settlements and industries, such as oil and mining.

Totems in Stanley Park, Vancouver

Amazon's headquarters

SEATTLE, in the United States, lies south of Vancouver. Ferry connections between the two cities take about seven hours via Victoria, on Vancouver Island. Seattle is a thriving, growing city with more than 720,000 people. In or near the city are the headquarters for major companies such as Microsoft and Amazon. The city attracts young people with good qualifications because of its booming economy, laid-back lifestyle, and the beautiful mountains and ocean nearby.

Pause for
REFLECTION

- In what ways do different cultures enrich cities like Vancouver and Seattle?
- How does the natural environment, including the landscape and resources, affect life in western coastal cities?

Road Trip Across CANADA

In Canada, most people live in the southern parts of the country, away from the icy Arctic region. The Trans-Canada Highway is a roadway that runs west and east across the country. Along the way, it cuts through the Rocky Mountains and crosses wide, flat prairies. It goes around the Great Lakes and passes through the eastern provinces of New Brunswick, Nova Scotia, Prince Edward Island, and Newfoundland and Labrador.

A ROAD TRIP on the Trans-Canada Highway takes travelers 4,860 miles (7,821 km), from British Columbia in the West to Newfoundland and Labrador in the East. The route is not all made up of roads. It includes one ferry crossing from Vancouver Island to the mainland, and one from Nova Scotia to Newfoundland and Labrador. The route includes the Confederation Bridge, which links New Brunswick to Prince Edward Island. The trip also requires a drive across the Canso **Causeway** that connects Nova Scotia's mainland to Cape Breton Island.

The Trans-Canada Highway

Rocky Mountains

Trans-Canada Highway

YUKON

NORTHWEST TERRITORIES

NUNAVUT

BRITISH COLUMBIA

ALBERTA

SASKATCHEWAN

MANITOBA

Hudson Bay

ONTARIO

QUEBEC

NEWFOUNDLAND AND LABRADOR

PRINCE EDWARD ISLAND

NEW BRUNSWICK

NOVA SCOTIA

Prince Rupert

Vancouver

Vancouver Island

Calgary

Winnipeg

Thunder Bay

Quebec City

Ottawa

Toronto

Sydney

Lumber truck, the Trans-Canada Highway

⬆ **TRANSPORT TRUCKS** use the Trans-Canada Highway to carry goods such as lumber. In areas with rugged landscapes, such as the Rocky Mountains and the **Canadian Shield**, workers blasted rock to carve a path for the highway. The route also provides a connection for many communities and a way for people to move east and west across the country. To keep up with travelers' changing needs, electric car charging stations are being installed along the Trans-Canada Highway. This also lessens the impact of traffic on the environment.

The Rideau Canal, Ottawa

PEOPLE ALONG THE WAY

The Pays Plat First Nation is a small community in Ontario. Its members regularly drive along the Trans-Canada Highway, crossing the Nipigon River Bridge to Thunder Bay. They shop there for fuel, food, and other supplies, as these are not available in their more isolated community. The highway is the only road that links the East and West. Thousands of cars and trucks use the route every day. The bridge closed for repairs for a time in 2016. This caused huge traffic jams on the highway, making everyday life very difficult for the Pays Plat people.

⬆ **OTTAWA** is the capital of Canada. The city lies towards the eastern end of the Trans-Canada Highway. It began as an important trading port for lumber, due to its central location for shipping. The Ottawa River connects to the St. Lawrence Seaway, a major transportation link between the Atlantic Ocean and the Great Lakes. The historic Rideau Canal passes through the heart of the city, with great views of the Canadian Parliament Buildings.

Dog Sledding in
GREENLAND

Greenland is the world's largest island. It is more than three times the size of the state of Texas. Even so, less than 60,000 people live there. On the map, Greenland belongs to North America, but it became a **colony** of Denmark in the eighteenth century. Today, Greenland is still part of Denmark, though it is mainly run separately. Some places are known by both Greenlandic and Danish names.

⬆ **COVERED BY A LARGE ICE CAP,** much of Greenland is uninhabitable, or not suitable for living. Much of the land cannot be farmed, so food needs to be shipped or flown to the island. Most Greenlanders are Inuit. The largest group of Inuit are Kalaallit. Many people in Greenland live along the southwest coast in towns such as Ilulissat, where it is slightly warmer. Some people work in the fishing industry, because Greenland's main exports are shrimp and fish. There are no railroads and few roads in Greenland. People travel in vehicles adapted to the icy conditions, such as snowmobiles and dog sleds. They use boats, helicopters, or airplanes for longer journeys.

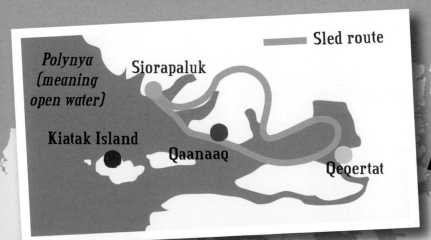

Sled route

Polynya (meaning open water)

Siorapaluk

QAANAAQ (THULE)

GREENLAND

Kiatak Island

Qaanaaq

Qeqertat

ILULISSAT

Houses in Qaanaaq

◄ THE TOWN OF QAANAAQ

is also known as Thule. Located in northwest Greenland, the tiny port town sits along a **fjord**. Temperatures stay below freezing for nine months of the year. In Qaanaaq, and in other communities, there are colorful wooden buildings. Most sit on stilts to keep the **permafrost** underneath from melting. There are very few trees on Greenland, so builders import the lumber to ports such as Qaanaaq. Greenland also depends on imports of food, fuel, and other supplies. Most of this comes by airplane or ship from Denmark.

Climate change is having a big effect on Greenland. The thick ice cap is slowly melting and the sea is frozen for less of the year. This threatens animals and the livelihoods of hunters. The shorter winters mean that they can no longer hunt safely far out on the sea ice.

↓ DOG SLEDDING for transportation and hunting is still

important to Kalaallit culture. The Kalaallit have used dog sleds for about 5,000 years. At a young age, children start learning the art of "mushing," or commanding the sled dogs. Many Kalaallit rely on **subsistence** hunting, and they move around Greenland to find food. Dog sleds allow them to reach areas that modern vehicles could not. Today, the Kalaallit also take tourists on dog sled journeys over Greenland's frozen landscape. This is one of the best ways to see parts of Greenland that are impossible to visit otherwise. The money from tourism helps to boost the local economy.

A dog sled tour

PEOPLE ALONG THE WAY

Aquingwak is an Inuit hunter who lives in Qaanaaq. He takes his dog sleds to go hunting and fishing. He makes money by selling some of his catch, but he also uses the animals for food and clothing. He adds to his earnings with dog sled tours for tourists.

Streetcar Around TORONTO

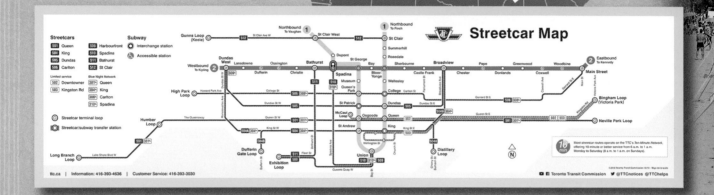

Toronto is Canada's largest city. Almost 3 million people live there. More than 3 million more live in the areas surrounding the city, known as the Greater Toronto Area (GTA). Toronto is a major financial and cultural center located on the north shore of Lake Ontario. This location, with easy access to the St. Lawrence Seaway and the United States, attracted millions of people, helping Toronto to grow into a modern, **cosmopolitan** city.

▼ **TORONTO'S STREETCARS** are vital to many people, including **commuters** and visitors to the city. The streetcar and other city transportation systems, such as subways and buses, connect different neighborhoods, including Little Italy and Greektown. Most of the routes run 24 hours a day. The 501 Queen Street route is the longest streetcar route in North America. It carries more than 40,000 passengers every day across the city.

A Toronto streetcar

BY LAKE ONTARIO, the 501 streetcar stops in "The Beaches." Here, people enjoy swimming, beach games, and walking along the shore. The lake also provides drinking water for millions of people in Toronto and elsewhere. However, the many cities, farms, and industries around the lake have caused high levels of pollution. Governments and environmental groups are working to restore and protect the lake's clean water. For example, Toronto plans to improve the treatment of wastewater from the city.

"The Beaches," Lake Ontario

Polish festival, Toronto

TORONTO'S VIBRANT CULTURE is a result of the huge mix of people who have moved there from all around the world. Almost half the people who live in Toronto were born outside of Canada, and about 200 languages are spoken in the city. Many form communities in particular neighborhoods. For example, in the west, the 501 route goes through Roncesvalles. Polish **immigrants** have brought their food and culture to this area. Every September, the neighborhood hosts the largest Polish festival in North America. There are many other festivals every year in Toronto, including a Caribbean carnival, and outdoor music festivals.

PEOPLE ALONG THE WAY

Wayne has been a streetcar driver for eight years. He enjoys the 501 Queen Street route because he meets many people who cross the city to get to work. The commuters come from different backgrounds, just like Wayne's family. Wayne has relatives in China and Jamaica. His wife was born in Colombia. Many of his passengers are regular travelers, but he sees newcomers every day.

Barge on the MISSISSIPPI

The Mississippi River flows from Lake Itasca, Minnesota, to the Gulf of Mexico at Louisiana. Its length is 2,320 to 2,552 miles (3,733 to 4,107 km), depending on the year and how it is measured. It passes through 10 states. Many other rivers, from small streams to large, important rivers such as the Missouri and Arkansas Rivers, flow into the Mississippi. These are called **tributaries**. They form river highways across the central United States.

Native Americans used the Mississippi and its tributaries to travel and carry goods for trade. The river was a good source of food—from fishing—and fresh water. As European settlers moved up the river, they farmed, and built cities and ports.

Minneapolis
Saint Louis
Memphis
New Orleans

Mississippi River and some of its tributaries

↓ SAINT PAUL AND MINNEAPOLIS are "twin" cities not far from the source of the river. They are the starting point of many barge journeys from the port terminal of Saint Paul. As the two cities grew, they became one large, **metropolitan** area. The Mississippi River connects these northern cities to those in the South. River barges carry millions of tons of **freight** every year.

A barge near Minneapolis

↓ THE PORT OF SOUTH LOUISIANA,

the end of many barge journeys, is the busiest cargo port in North America. Thousands of people work at the port, on the barges, and on the ships. The port stretches along 54 miles (87 km) of the Mississippi River near New Orleans. Goods such as grain, petroleum, iron, and wood ship to and from the port. Cargo ships travel by sea to 90 other countries around the world, including Russia, Brazil, and China.

Barge loading, Port of South Louisiana

Flood rescue, New Orleans

↑ LONG AFTER THE ABOLISHMENT OF SLAVERY,

New Orleans is still a diverse mixture of French, Spanish, African, and Native American influences. New Orleans first attracted settlers because of its location at the Mississippi **Delta**, where the river flows into the Gulf of Mexico. European settlers took land from the Native Americans of the area. Through slavery, they also forced African people to help build the city, and to work on the land around it.

New Orleans lies on low land close to the sea, which puts it at risk of flooding. Hurricane Katrina devastated the city in 2005. More than a thousand people died, while thousands of others lost their homes. The hurricane forced many to move away from the city permanently, and it took many years to repair the damage.

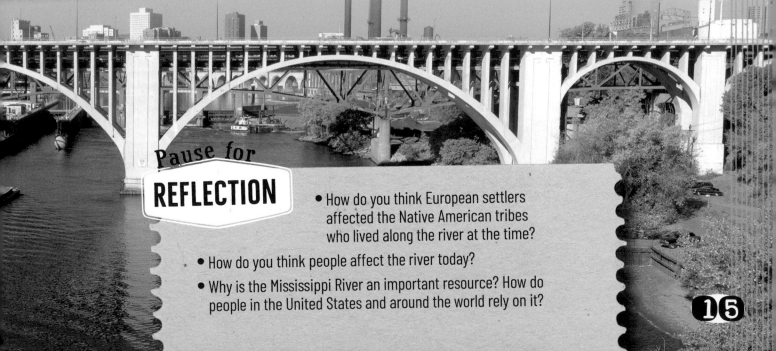

Pause for
REFLECTION

- How do you think European settlers affected the Native American tribes who lived along the river at the time?

- How do you think people affect the river today?

- Why is the Mississippi River an important resource? How do people in the United States and around the world rely on it?

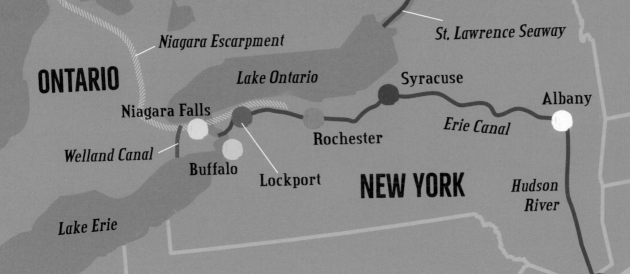

ONTARIO

Niagara Escarpment

St. Lawrence Seaway

Lake Ontario

Syracuse

Albany

Niagara Falls

Erie Canal

Rochester

Welland Canal

NEW YORK

Buffalo

Lockport

Hudson River

Lake Erie

New York City

Boat Cruise on the ERIE CANAL

In the nineteenth century, the Erie Canal was one of the most important human-made waterways in North America, and a gateway to the Great Lakes. Used today mainly for leisure and tourism, the canal runs 363 miles (584 km), from the Hudson River near Albany in the state of New York to close to Buffalo on Lake Erie. Come for a cruise along it.

Barge on the Erie Canal, 1890s

◄⋯ **THE ERIE CANAL** opened in 1825. For the first time, there was a water route for people and goods to travel quickly and cheaply between New York City and areas west of the Appalachian Mountains. The same journey took weeks over land. There was so much traffic that engineers have since made the canal larger and deeper. The success of the Erie Canal led to the building of other canals, such as the Welland Canal in Ontario, Canada, that connects Lake Ontario to Lake Erie.

ENGINEERS AND BUILDERS dealt with many challenges to build the canal, including mountains, dangerous river rapids, and thick forests. Originally, the boats moved through 83 **locks**. Today, there are 35. At the Niagara **Escarpment**, they built five wide locks to raise and lower boats by 60 feet (18 m). Some of the canal builders settled here, forming the town of Lockport. At Buffalo, the canal meets Lake Erie. From there, goods were shipped west through the Great Lakes.

The canal continued to be important until the opening of railway routes in the later 1800s and the St. Lawrence Seaway in the 1950s. Today, it is mainly tourists that take boat journeys along the Erie Canal itself, but cargo ships move through the Welland Canal. This has eight locks that allow ships to move up and down the Niagara Escarpment, between Lake Erie and Lake Ontario.

A cargo ship on the Welland Canal

Pause for
REFLECTION

- How did the canal affect communities along its route?
- What negative effects on land or people may have come from the building of the canal?
- Is it a good idea to keep the canal open for tourists? Why or why not?

The Statue of Liberty by the New York City skyline

CITIES such as Syracuse, Rochester, and Buffalo were created with the opening of the Erie Canal, as it helped more people to settle in these areas. The canal also helped to make New York one of the most important cities in the United States. It was a major port for arriving immigrants. Many then went up the Hudson River to the Erie Canal to travel west. The canal also opened a major trade route, enabling New York to grow into a financial center. This attracted even more people to the city.

Fly Out of ATLANTA

ATLANTA

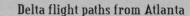

Let's fly from New York into Hartsfield-Jackson Atlanta International Airport, the busiest passenger airport in the world. In 2017, almost 104 million people passed through the airport, or about 275,000 people per day. People travel by air for many reasons, including vacations, work, and to relocate. In North America, including the United States and Canada, air travel is especially important because of the long distances between major cities.

▼ **DELTA AIRLINES,** one of the world's largest airlines, operates out of Atlanta. Delta and other corporations, such as Coca-Cola, have their headquarters in the city. Good flight connections help make Atlanta an attractive location for large businesses. These corporations in turn bring thousands of people to the city to work and live.

Delta airplanes at the Atlanta airport

The Light Tunnel in the Atlanta airport

▶ THE AIRPORT COMPLEX covers 156.1 acres (63.2 hectares). Travelers and airport staff move around this huge area using the colorful underground Light Tunnel and train links. The airport is the state of Georgia's largest employer. More than 63,000 people work there. Atlanta became such a busy airport because it is within about a two-hour flight of most other major U.S. cities. Many people fly to Atlanta only to connect with another flight.

A busy highway, Atlanta

◀ ATLANTA'S strong economy, its warm climate, and location have made it one of the fastest-growing places in North America. Many people also live in its sprawling **suburbs**. The city's rail and bus links, and its road network, have not grown quickly enough to cope with the number of people. This has caused problems with road traffic. The local environment can suffer from poor air quality as a result.

Atlanta's population growth has also put pressure on its water supplies. This has been made worse by frequent **droughts**. The local water suppliers encourage people to use less water by raising the water charges for high usage.

PEOPLE ALONG THE WAY

Cheryl works as a passenger assistant at the Atlanta airport, helping travelers in wheelchairs. She has no car, and lives in a suburb of Atlanta that has no bus. She has to pay for a taxi to get to work. She waits for an hour after work so she can ride home with a friend. She hopes to save enough money to buy her own car. On her current wage, this will take time.

Going WEST by Train

In the United States and Canada, the first railroads were built in the 1800s. The trains made it much easier to travel long distances and carry cargo. This brought settlers to the western United States. Communities grew near the railway routes, and some of the largest cities in the United States can be found along train routes. Let's take a trip on the *California Zephyr* rail route—one of the most dramatic in the world.

NORTH DAKOTA

SOUTH DAKOTA

IOWA

Chicago

Emeryville

Salt Lake City

NEBRASKA

NEVADA

Denver

INDIANA

San Francisco

UTAH

COLORADO

KANSAS

ILLINOIS

MISSOURI

CALIFORNIA

Rocky Mountains

Corn Belt

▼ **THE *CALIFORNIA ZEPHYR*** begins in Chicago, Illinois. It journeys west across plains, deserts, and mountains. It travels more than 2,400 miles (3,862 km) to Emeryville, near San Francisco, California. The whole trip will take just over two days, or 51 hours. Many tourists ride the train, attracted by the scenery and the opportunity to visit cities along the way.

EUROPEAN SETTLERS were among the first people to travel the railroad. The governments of Canada and the United States encouraged them to go west by offering them land. However, this land was already inhabited by Indigenous peoples. The governments forced these nations to leave their land and live in areas called reservations in the United States, or reserves, in Canada.

These Indigenous peoples not only lost their land but also their traditional way of life, such as hunting bison. Instead, the settlers hunted these large grazing animals almost to the point of **extinction**. To build the railways and their settlements, the new arrivals also cleared large areas of forest for lumber. In this way, the railways completely changed the landscape of the West and the lives of its Indigenous peoples.

The *California Zephyr*, Utah

Railway tracks, Chicago

Pause for

REFLECTION

- This part of the United States has wide areas of grasslands, mountains, and deserts. What challenges would this geography have on people settling or moving through here?
- The railroad brought many people to the West. How has this affected the environment?
- What impact did western railway expansion in the United States and Canada have on Indigenous peoples?

⬆ **CHICAGO** sits at the southwestern tip of Lake Michigan, which made it an important shipping link. The city is the third largest in the country. It is also a major stop for freight trains. Half of the freight trains in the United States pass through here. West of Chicago, the train passes through the Corn Belt. Corn and other crops take up millions of acres of land in the Midwest. The railroad provides a way to transport the crops across the country. Corn production, however, comes at a cost. Over time, the fertilizers used in farming have polluted nearby rivers and lakes.

⬇ **LEAVING THE PLAINS** of the Corn Belt, the train crosses the mountains of the Rockies and the Sierra Nevada. To pass through the mountains, engineers dug tunnels and created pathways such as Donner Pass that cut through the rock. These pathways provide a vital connection between the areas east and west of the mountains.

The trip ends near San Francisco. The **Gold Rush** in the mid-1800s brought thousands of people to San Francisco and other western settlements, such as Denver. Because of the huge influx of people hoping to strike gold, small western communities quickly became large cities.

A train in the mountains

On Horseback Through the NAVAJO Territory

NAVAJO TERRITORY

UTAH

COLORADO

Monument Valley

Tuba City

ARIZONA

NEW MEXICO

Hopi Reservation
Navajo Reservation

The Navajo reservation is the largest in North America, with about 17.2 million acres (6.9 million hectares). Within its borders is the Hopi reservation, which has 1.5 million acres (607,000 hectares). You can see the landscape well on horseback. These reservations are two of 326 in the United States, while Canada has more than 3,000 reserves.

A rider on horseback in Monument Valley

▼ **MONUMENT VALLEY** is in the northwest region of the reservation. The area is a tribal park open to visitors, though some Navajo still live there and use the valley floor for farming. Today, the Navajo reservation lies here and on other parts of their traditional homeland in the western states of Arizona, Utah, and New Mexico. Much of the area is desert, but surrounding forests supply wood and have water. There are almost 14,500 farms on the reservation. People raise cattle and grow corn, beans, and alfalfa.

▶ THE NAVAJO ARE KNOWN FOR THE JEWELRY that they make and sell in Tuba City. Originally, the Navajo came to the area around Tuba City because of the natural underground springs, which supplied them with water. Tuba City became a trading center in the late 1800s. It is now the biggest settlement in the Navajo reservation.

From 1864 to 1866, the U.S. government forced more than 9,000 Navajo to move from their homeland. The "Long Walk of the Navajo" ended at a fort 450 miles (724 km) away. Along the way, many people died. The fort had little food or farmable land, and more than 2,000 Navajo died of hunger and disease. In 1868, the government allowed the surviving Navajo to return to part of their original land. Since 1923, the Navajo Nation has had its own government. It oversees the use of natural resources on the reservation, such as oil, uranium, and lumber.

A range of Navajo crafts

▼ A LARGE SOLAR FARM now powers 18,000 homes on the reservation. The Navajo have a very close relationship with the land. They have always depended on it for survival and know that it is important to protect it. One way of doing this is to use a renewable energy source such as the Sun. The desert is an ideal place to collect the Sun's energy.

PEOPLE
ALONG THE WAY

Jared has lived on the reservation all his life. He works as a guide to tourists. Outside of tourism and farming, there are few jobs available on the reservation. Many of Jared's friends have left their families to find work in cities such as Phoenix or Albuquerque. Jared hopes he can avoid leaving by maybe starting his own tour company one day.

Solar panels on the Navajo reservation

On the LOS ANGELES Metro

Los Angeles (or L.A.) began as a small, Spanish colony in the 1700s. Today, it is the second-largest city in the United States, after New York. It is a major manufacturing, financial, and entertainment center. The city lies on a large plain along the Pacific Ocean. This mostly flat land allowed Los Angeles to expand outward easily, as more people settled there.

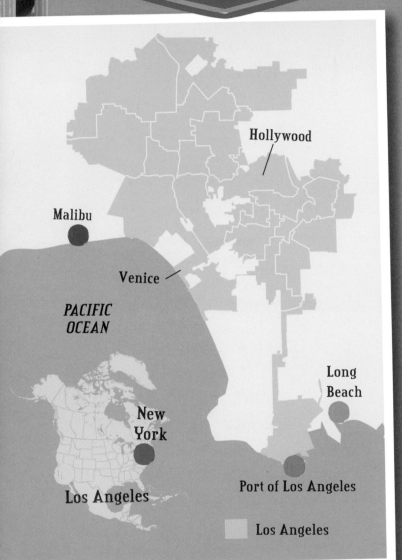

Los Angeles Metro train, Hollywood

⬆ **CAR TRAFFIC** is a constant problem in Los Angeles. Because there was a lot of space to build highways, Los Angeles was built for travel by car. One answer to traffic is the Metro rail system, which began operating in 1990. Since then, Los Angeles has continued to expand its public transportation system to deal with its growing population. The Metro is a combination of subway, or underground, rail lines and light, or overground, rail. The system takes passengers to and from major districts in L.A., such as Hollywood. It also includes stops just outside the city boundaries, such as Long Beach and Malibu.

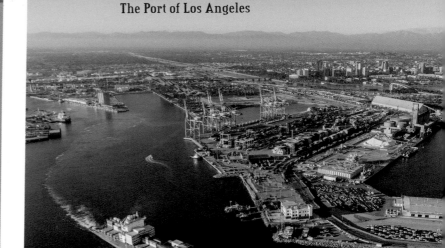
The Port of Los Angeles

↓ THE METRO BIKE SHARE SYSTEM

is another way to get around Los Angeles. The bicycles are linked to the subway system. People can pick up a Metro bike in areas such as Venice Beach or the Port of Los Angeles, use it, and drop it off at another location.

People have moved to Los Angeles to enjoy the southern California weather and to work in the large manufacturing and entertainment industries there. However, the city's location and climate change mean that earthquakes, extreme heat, rising sea levels, and wildfires are concerns for the people living there. The wildfires around Los Angeles in 2018 were very bad because of the dry and windy weather conditions.

Metro bike stands, Los Angeles

The Los Angeles skyline

↑ THE PORT OF LOS ANGELES sits

on the Pacific Ocean. It is the busiest **container** port in North America. The port takes up 43 miles (69 km) along the shore, and employs more than 147,000 people in Los Angeles. The port accepts import shipments from Asia, such as cars and clothing. Exports of paper, soybeans, and many other goods leave from here to cross the Pacific Ocean back to Asia.

Pause for
REFLECTION

- Why do you think it took so long for Los Angeles to get a subway system?
- What things can Los Angeles do to help deal with climate change?
- How do you think the city's huge expansion has affected the environment?

Every day, transport trucks travel the Pan-American Highway. They carry goods within Mexico and Central America. Some trucks travel north to the United States and Canada. The highway is not a single road. Instead, it is a system of roads that links Canada, the United States, Mexico, and Central America. There is a gap in the network in a jungle area of southern Panama, before it continues into South America.

▼ **TRANSPORT TRUCKS** use the highway to take their goods to the U.S.-Mexico border at Laredo, Texas. These trucks carry Mexican exports such as computers, cars, fruits, and vegetables. Laredo is also a place where millions of Mexican immigrants have entered the United States. They often look for work in California and Texas. As Mexico's economy has grown stronger, fewer people leave Mexico to find work. However, the U.S.–Mexico border is still a busy place for human migration. Thousands of **asylum seekers** from Central America travel through Mexico to the U.S. border. Most are escaping violence in their home countries.

The Pan-American Highway,
northern Mexico

Trucking on the PAN-AMERICAN Highway

Whitehorse

CANADA

Vancouver

Thunder Bay

Butte

Minneapolis

UNITED STATES OF AMERICA

Kansas City

Las Vegas

Denver

Los Angeles

San Diego

El Paso

San Antonio

MEXICO

Laredo

Monterrey

Mexico City

Guatemala City

Mexico City skyline

⬇ **MONTERREY,** south of the U.S. border, has grown up partly because of its position on the highway. This gives it good transportation connections to ports in the United States and Mexico, attracting businesses from throughout Mexico and around the world. Mexicans and people from other countries come to work and study in the city. Outside the city are automobile and auto parts manufacturers. The auto industry has become very important for Mexico, and it employs many people. Most cars are exported to the U.S. and Canada. Factories have brought jobs to Monterrey, but the area's growth has led to widespread **deforestation**.

Car factory worker, Monterrey

⬆ **MEXICO CITY** is farther south down the Pan-American Highway. It is the largest city in North America. More than 21 million people live in the city and its surrounding area. It was built on the ruins of the Aztec capital city of Tenochtitlán, in a large valley surrounded by mountains. Mexico City lies in the center of the country, with trade routes in all directions.

PEOPLE

ALONG THE WAY

Eduardo is a truck driver based in Monterrey. In his truck, Eduardo carries household appliances, such as refrigerators. These will end up in kitchens across the United States. Eduardo spends up to 18 hours a day driving up and down the highway. The long days are hard, but Eduardo knows he has a secure job with a regular wage.

Panama City

MEXICO

BELIZE

GUATEMALA

HONDURAS

EL SALVADOR

NICARAGUA

Shipping Out of COSTA RICA

To Canada and the United States

CARIBBEAN SEA

To Canada, the United States, and Asia

COSTA RICA

Limón

To Europe

San José

Panama Canal

Caldera

PANAMA

PACIFIC OCEAN

To South America

Shipping route

Costa Rica is a small, narrow country in Central America, located between the Pacific Ocean to the west and the Caribbean Sea to the east. Costa Rica's high mountains and dense forests mean there are few roads, so shipping in and out of coastal ports is vital to the country. Most of the population lives in the central valley, on a high **plateau**, which includes the capital city, San José. Costa Rica has a good economy, giving its people more jobs and better education than most Central American countries. This has attracted many immigrants from neighboring countries.

▼ **AGRICULTURE** is an important industry in Costa Rica. The country is a leading exporter of bananas, pineapples, and coffee. In 2017, Costa Rica exported bananas to China for the first time. This cargo left the country from the Port of Caldera, on the Pacific Ocean. In recent years, medical equipment, such as scanners, has also become a key export. This kind of export has become more common, thanks to the government's support of high-tech industries.

Costa Rican bananas

THE PORT OF LIMÓN on the Caribbean Sea is Costa Rica's largest port. Like Caldera, freight and cruise ships come in and out of this port. Costa Rica is a top tourist destination for its natural beauty, including long beaches on the coasts and spectacular mountains. The country has reversed deforestation and protected a quarter of its land and animals with national parks and wildlife reserves. Although Costa Rica's landscape is beautiful, earthquakes and active volcanoes can be a problem. The ash from eruptions causes damage to crops and can force the airports to close. Earthquakes can cut off electricity and topple buildings.

A hiker beneath a Costa Rican volcano

Ships on the Panama Canal

PANAMA, a neighboring country to the south, imports many goods from Costa Rica. Panama is on an **isthmus** that connects North America to South America, another continent. In the early 1900s, the United States built the Panama Canal, which cuts through the land and connects the Atlantic and Pacific Oceans. Panama expanded the canal in 2016 so that larger ships could pass through it. The United States and China are the chief users of the canal, which is one of the world's most important shipping links.

Pause for REFLECTION

- How would reversing deforestation help Costa Rica's economy?

- How does the country's landscape affect its settlement?

- How do Costa Rica and other Central American countries depend on international trade?

GLOSSARY

asylum seekers People who have left their own country and are asking permission to live in another country for political reasons

Canadian Shield Large, rocky area underlying about half of Canada's land

causeway A raised road, often over wet ground

climate change Change in climate patterns around the world due to global warming, or the gradual increase in Earth's temperature

climates The usual weather conditions of regions over a long period of time

colony A land or region controlled and settled by another country

commuter A person who regularly travels, usually some distance, to and from work and home

container A large metal box, usually of a standard size, used to transport goods by ship, rail, and truck

cosmopolitan Describes a place that has people from different parts of the world

deforestation Clearing trees to use the land for human purposes, such as farming

delta A D-shaped area of flat land, often marshy, where a river or rivers empty into an ocean or sea

droughts Long periods of time with little or no rain

economy The system by which goods and services are made, sold, bought, and used

escarpment A steep, long cliff

exported Goods sent to be sold in another country

extinction Describes when a species of animal or plant dies out completely

First Nations Name used to describe a specific Indigenous group, or nation, in Canada

fjord Narrow section of sea between high cliffs or hills

freight Goods transported in bulk

Gold Rush Movement of people sparked by the discovery of gold in California in 1848

Ice Age A period of colder climate conditions when Earth's ice sheets covered large areas of its surface

immigrant Person who comes to live in a country from another country

imported Goods brought into a country to be sold

Indigenous Describes people who naturally exist or live in a place rather than arrived from elsewhere

industries All of the people and businesses involved in making or providing certain goods and services

isthmus Narrow piece of land that connects to larger land areas

locks Sections on a canal with gates that control the level of water so as to raise and lower boats

metropolitan Describes a large city and its surrounding areas

natural resources Useful or valuable materials and substances in nature, such as trees or gold

permafrost Thick layer of land that is frozen all year round

plateau An area of mainly flat, high ground

reservation Area of land in the United States set aside for Indigenous people to live

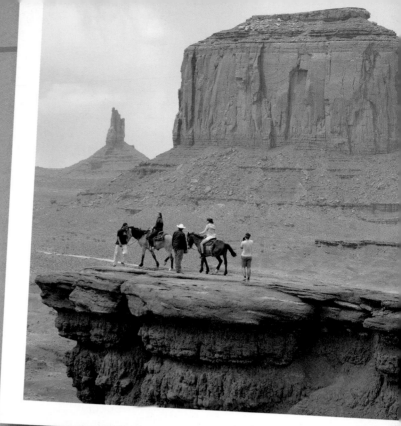

reserve Area of land in Canada set aside for First Nations to live. Few Inuit and Metis live on reserves, but they may live in self-governed settlements.

settlers People who have come to live permanently, or settle, in a place from somewhere else

subsistence Hunting only the amount of food needed to stay alive, but not enough to sell to others

suburbs Areas surrounding a city where people live

treaty Official agreement between two or more groups—in this case, a government and an Indigenous nation

tributaries Streams or rivers that flow into a larger river or lake

Further INFORMATION

BOOKS

Cooke, Tim. *Mapping Human Activity*. Crabtree Publishing, 2017.

Nelson, Maria. *The Pan-American Highway*. Gareth Stevens, 2016.

Rockett, Paul. *Mapping North America*. Crabtree Publishing, 2017.

Whipple, Annette. *North America*. Rourke Educational Media, 2018.

WEBSITES

www.nationalgeographic.org/encyclopedia/north-america-human-geography/
This website provides a general guide to North American geography and people.

www.akgtcanada.com Check out an interactive guide to Canada made by kids for kids, with teacher input.

kids.nationalgeographic.com/explore/countries/united-states/
This website provides an overview of the United States, from its physical geography to its varied economy.

kids.nationalgeographic.com/explore/countries/mexico/
Learn about Mexico, from its people and culture to its history.

INDEX

ABOUT THE AUTHOR

Cynthia O'Brien has lived and worked in Canada and England. She has made many different journeys across North America and elsewhere. She has written many books, including stories of explorers, lost treasures, and cultures around the world.